Family Secrets and Then Some

Breaking Generational Curses

JJ Snipes

Table of Contents

Dedication

This book is dedicated to my baby girl Meina LaMere, My sons Jonah, Jasiel, And Johnathan (Chew Chew) Snipes, my 3 mothers Aunt Sissy, Aunt Lydia, and Mom. I want to thank my sister Pauline for always believing in me and pushing me to be the man I am today, I love you, sis. Uncle Lefty, you were the best Dad ever even though I didn't realize it at the time I love you and I'm forever grateful for your tough love. A special thanks to Lina "Beanie" Williams, you inspired me.

Acknowledgment

I must thank God for the heart that he gave me, for the grace and mercy that He has bestowed on my life, and for the dreams, He put in my heart. I am grateful to all that have loved and supported me throughout my journey. I also must give a shout out to Ms. Oprah Winfrey. In one of her speeches, she said "Before you do anything, ask yourself. What is your intention? I'm telling my story to help people, but my intentions were to be seen also. Which was not pure. So, I am rewriting my book and correcting my intentions. Someone out there will understand and see how God pulled me up out of the muck and mire. Never doubt that God is there, and everything happens for a reason.

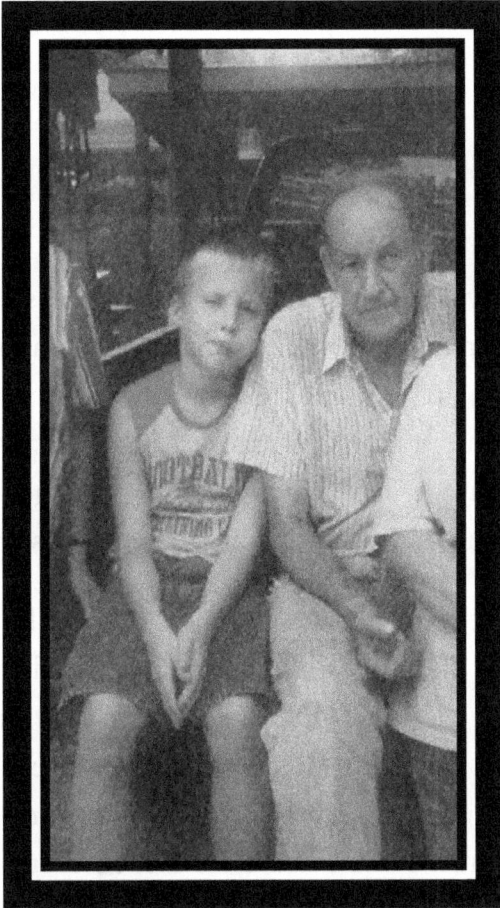

JJ & Uncle Lefty

Preface

This story is about a child severely oppressed by the generational curse, which was taken as a standard of living in his childhood. He has witnessed abandonment from his parents since his childhood, by which he gets paranoid and indulges in life destructing drugs and eventually escalates over it.

Meanwhile, as certainty over being an abundant kid, his aunt and uncle fulfilled every aspect of his life with firm diligence by which he has been generous all his future ventures, yet the dilemma of being observing the symptoms of the generational curse haunts him back then, and he has had to deal with immense trauma throughout his life.

Although he interacted into something taken as a *Taboo*, this is something that primitively affected his life and by which JJ has learned from worldly things. He is a Gemini and possesses a spiritual gift from God.that made him distinctive from others and opened doors of understanding missing pieces of his life with prompt conviction.

Moreover, this book is entitled about the gray shades of Generational curses and specifically concerning the new generation that will suffer the hardships of these kinds of traumas and helps them to propagate hope and self-love. In contrast with the cruel calamity of life, it provides a healthy upbringing to protect them by exposing the cruelty of this world despite being embarrassed. The affirmation on what God's plan is always best for you, it will take time to heal with the trauma, but soon everything falls into place.

Chapter 1
The Road to Healing

Today, I was sitting in my truck, thinking of Uncle Lefty. I will never forget the afternoon that I went to his house, the house I grew up in, and we were sitting out by the barbecue pit, and he answered all the questions that I have had for most of my life. As we sat there shooting the shit, he looked at me, and he said it's time for you to know some things. It was a warm afternoon in Jacksonville, Florida. I have to say this. My uncle was from Carrie West Virginia and normally did not speak like that, best said God works in mysterious ways.

He and my Aunt Sissy raised me, and they gave me the best of everything," spoiled " did not even come close to what I was growing up. Aunt Sissy Gave Me Everything. The best clothes, the best schools, etc. I was seventeen. I had three vehicles; it was insane, they did not have much growing up and she wanted to give me a better life the best way she knew how. It was normal that I lived with them. I never asked any questions. Mom wasn't in the picture. I just went on every day at this thing we call life. This day was different; he told me a few things. He asked me about my job, and how it was going, I told him I had been promoted, he grinned.

See, throughout my life, I thought he hated me. Whenever I cut the grass, washed his truck, or stacked the firewood. It was never good enough; if I missed a spot while washing his truck, he would make me wash it over; if the wood wasn't stacked how he wanted it stacked, he would kick it over and make me do it again. I honestly believed this man hated me and wished me dead, but I could not have been further from the truth. He made me a competitive person; I was the best at whatever I did. No one could beat me. He showed me love well. They would call it tough love, but it was love. He made me the man that you're looking at today. He continued to tell me that day that the reason they were raising me or that they raised me was because Mom was at one of her two or three jobs, or she was in a bar.

My mom loved my dad; they were together for a while. They loved shooting pool and dancing. She always said what a good man he was. Then, she found out that he was married to a woman in Georgia. So, she broke it off. She couldn't see herself dating a man who was married. It broke her heart. I met my dad when I was 15. He pulled up in this big black 1963 Lincoln, I do not know how I knew, but I knew he was my daddy. The way they looked at each other was magical. It had been at least 11 years since they had seen each other.

He was killed in an accident when I was 21, and I found out that he was still married to that woman in Georgia. When he left her in 1970. He never went back. His intentions with my mother were pure.

Throughout my teenage years and early 20s up into my thirties, I had drug addictions. I had mommy and daddy issues. I never understood why mom would not let me stay with her. I don't even remember her until I'm between 10 and 12 years old. The conversation that he and I had that day explained it all. He didn't hate me. He just wanted me to be a man, and he understood what the world was coming to and that I would have had to be competitive because as spoiled as I was, he knew I would have issues.

The abandonment issues still affect me to this day, but I have forgiven myself, and I forgave my mom & dad because one thing about mommies and daddies, they're human. They make mistakes. I wish mine would have healed earlier in life. She was 79 years old when I taught her about shadow work, but it is never too late.

God has touched my life, well touched doesn't even come close to describing what He has brought me through. If you're being challenged by life right now, just know that He is real and if you just trust and believe, I promise He will guide and see you through anything. Mathew 7:7 says "Ask, and it will be given to you; seek, and you will find; knock and it shall be opened." In a nutshell keep on asking, and you will receive what you ask for.

Keep seeking and you will find it. Knock and the door will be opened for you.

God is our Father; we are His children. Just reach out in faith and take His hand. He will fix it. Jesus will fix it.

Chapter 2
The Apple Doesn't Fall Too Far from The Tree

When I was twelve, I walked into the living room, my mom was sitting in her chair, and the anger was boiling out of her. I didn't understand my gift at the time. I am an intuitive empath, so I was feeling her energy. She stayed mad. The pattern for generations was "No Love". I have heard my mom and her siblings say. My grandmother never hugged them, never expressed any love or affection throughout their lives. My Great Grandmother was an evil woman, from what I hear. When I was 7, my aunt told me we were going to the funeral home to see her, and I asked her why? She told me. " So, I can pinch the bitch, to make sure she's dead." I never understood their hate for Miss Raker, just another one of those generational curses.

The story is that Miss Raker was "Madam Raker". She ran a whorehouse; my great aunts were sold starting at the age of 12 years old. My Paw Paw bought my grandmother before Ms. Raker could turn her into a whore. I was told that whenever my grandmother was two years old that my great grandmother (Miss Raker) poured a pan of hot chicken grease on her head. Throughout my grandmother's life, she had brain surgeries, etc, she also had a lung removed.

All the stories that I have heard about how hateful my grandmother was, they say she was a giving woman. She would give you her last. My mom told me one time that this lady was at their house, and she commented that she liked a lamp that my grandmother had. Phoebie (my grandmother's name) gave it to her. My mom and Aunt Sissy are just like her.

I am told that I have her heart, but her temper made her a feared woman also, so it seems. Throughout the years, as I said, she had to have surgeries on her head. My Pawpaw worked for the school board. They had six kids. The last time that Granny was in the hospital. Pawpaw could not keep them, so Miss Raker had them put into a home where they were abused. My mom and her siblings assume that Miss Raker did this out of spite. I have a spiritual gift, and we'll get to that later, but I have communicated with Miss Raker, and it wasn't that at all. She wanted to, let's say that whenever granny found out, she fought hard to get well and got out of the hospital and got the kids. It's a shame that hate and no love and affection can pass from generation to generation. Aunt Sissy started breaking one of the generational curses. She showed affection and love to me.

It all started with me; my mom told me she loved me for the first time when I was 17. I was in the hospital because I had a near overdose on drugs. She never hugged us or showed any affection... Sound familiar? Later, I started working on her, and it started changing gradually and growing up with Aunt Sissy and Uncle Lefty. I always got love from Aunt Sissy. I kissed her on the cheek every night before going to bed, so I was used to being affectionate, and Aunt Sissy had started early on breaking the generational curse.

She's never talked about it and won't talk about her spiritual gift, but she's a See'er also, (A see'er is a person who prophesies future events; a person endowed with profound moral and spiritual insight or knowledge: a wise person or sage who posseses intuitive powers.

Chapter 3
The Struggle

It was July 2017, and I left the house with my newborn son, I would usually ride around with Jasiel to quiet him down, but today was different. I was online talking to an acquaintance, and he invited me over so his mother could see my son. My new baby boy, but intern, met the love of my life and the destruction of my life. I was drawn like a moth to a flame. It was one of the most amazing days of my life thus far.

I got a text one day and went and picked him up. Mari's energy was insane. I felt like we had known each other for a lifetime. Hé was like a whirlwind that came in and took over my life, my senses... It was just mind-blowing. It wasn't the first time we had been together, though; we had done this in another lifetime.

When I say took me by storm. The first few minutes together. I knew our souls knew each other. It was an attraction like nothing I had ever felt that first day. We had a couple of drinks, and we spent time together for a while and got acquainted. We laughed, and it felt like long lost love had been reignited.

After everything we have gone through, I can think about that day. I still get butterflies, and it brings a smile to my face. It was just magical. I never understood the hold that this relationship, friendship, situation ship, whatever you want to call it, had on me. So, I had a past life regression reading done. I found out that we had been together 783 years before,

It was around the year 1234 in Antwerp Belgium. He was 18 and I was 16. He was in the upper class, and I was in the lower class. It was forbidden love. The families did not approve of this engagement. Especially his father. Even then it was like a whirl wind romance.

One day I was out for a walk and 2 men came up and grabbed me, held me down and put shackles on my ankles with a polygon shaped iron and tossed me off of a cliff and into the river. Death was instantaneous.

He never married after my death, he had chances to, but he didn't. It was eternal love. He thought my death was an accident, but it was murder, that his father had ordered.

They say True love never dies. Mine never did. I loved him from the moment I laid eyes on him.

(Eternal Love) is the title of my future book.

Wow... It turned into a passion. My soul recognized his; it was screaming out. I knew he was mine for life. It wasn't just a physical attraction. My soul had to have his. This love wasn't about lust. It was Love in its deepest since. It confused him how I didn't want to ravish him sexually; all he knew was showing affection through sex. He was taught there was no such thing as love. That is how most of us who were sexually abused are. The only thing that satisfies us is what traumatized us as a child. Deep down in our subconscious, we do what was done to us, to please whoever we are with. We stay in the mindset of pleasing our tormentor, unknowingly. Only 5% of our actions in life come from our conscious mind. 95% comes from the subconscious.

That's why it is so important not to shame your children, and repeat all of the childhood traumas, projecting them to our children and continuing the generational curse.

You will find throughout life that many types of soulmates will come along. Some are just a friend, some are karmic, and others are real soulmates, but they are merely damaged from what they have been through in this life. That's what happened to us. We could not deny the connection, but I was healing, he refused to.

If two people fall in love in one life, they become soulmates. You will find. That usually you will run into the person in another life and whenever you meet them your souls already know each other. The brain doesn't recognize them, but your soul does. I know you have met someone, whether it's just a friend and it feels like you've known them all your life, it's probably because you have known them in a past life.

Love can make you lose yourself. You get so involved, and being the person that I am, a giver. If I love you, I will let you know every day; I would attribute that to the abandonment issues I have. It's sad how our traumas affect how we love. In some cases, we come off as needy or desperate, when all We want is to show you the love that we've always hungered for throughout our lives. I'm still a loving person; it's just who I am. I learned a valuable lesson this year. It's not your job to fix what you didn't break, and many of us spend our lives trying to do just that. If you didn't break it, you can't put it back together; they need to heal, and that is all that is going to fix it. So, in 2019, whenever I cut my fingers off and found out that God was in control, I started working on myself. I started paying attention and watching motivational speakers, doing better for myself, and working on the way I act and react to situations, but the main thing I've done is set boundaries. It took me a couple of years after this time in my life; I finally stopped being a push over. I stopped allowing people to use me Because most of the time that my phone rang, it was someone asking, can you, will you, do you ... It's like the only time that they call you is whenever they want something, and I had to put a stop to it.

Chapter 4
The Wake-Up Call

2019 was a crazy year. In July of that year, I was helping a friend of mine; we were remodeling a bathroom. While working on the floor, we also had to jack the house up.

I went outside to cut some wedges and ended up cutting off my four-finger and thumb. I can still hear the noise. The pop, pop, pop sound was my finger hitting the saw blade and looking down at my fingers; I lost it. This could not happen to me; my friend Mark went into Superman mode, got me in the truck, and rushed me to the hospital. I called my mom and told her What had happened, but I started getting weak. I remember jumping the curb in the truck; I felt it because he was driving, and everything started getting bright. Just imagine the sun intensifying fifty thousand times. I could feel myself going up; there was no panic, and there was no pain, just peace.

You know how it feels when you're going up a roller coaster whenever it first starts, and you're going up the embankment right before you drop off.

That's what it felt like; I couldn't stop it. I had no control; I just had to go with the flow. The next thing I remember, I was waking up in the hospital, and I asked the doctor why it got so bright, and he told me "You were leaving us - son." That stuck with me for a while. You see the arrogant, narcissistic ways I had; I thought I was invincible. I had the attitude that I was Superman, and nothing could hurt me or take me down.

Well, God reached down to let me know that day that I wasn't invincible, that death was real, and that's when my eyes began to open. My life started changing that day. Have you ever had Precision Focus?

I started listening to motivational tapes on YouTube channels and thinking about being a keynote speaker. I have a story, and I believe that it can help people. I used to wonder why I went through the things that I went through, and now I do not question it because I vow to use my pain to help heal others thatare going through the same thing that I've been through.

Chapter 5
Decisions

In 2016 I was going through a rough time. Hurricane Mathew hit Florida. I walked away from the security company and started working. I started in St. Augustine as a monitor for a large company out of Orlando Florida. I did very well and was considered for promotion in the second week. Unfortunately, one of the companies ran a background check and refused to promote me.

My supervisor made an executive decision and promoted me anyhow; it was like I was made for it. During the first week, I was monitoring a truck. Now, what I mean by monitoring. FEMA sends us out as the accountants for them. We document what debris the trucks pick up and haul to the dump. As I was working this day, I observed an older woman about 80 years old.

She was in a lawn chair in her front yard. I thought nothing of it and finished the day as usual. The following morning, I arrived back at the same house we were working on the day before, and I noticed her sitting in the same spot.

As I walked over to her, I asked her if she was okay. She told me that She had no one Her children We're in another state, and an insurance man had sold her hurricane insurance which covered the roof, but it didn't cover floods, her house, along with about 800 other houses, had been flooded and the water went up about 5 ft in the house. I called my supervisor, and we then contacted the Red Cross And got her some assistance; I decided that day that this is what I was supposed to be doing. I started my mission.

I took off, and within a year and a half and three states later, I was appointed as an assistant project manager. Thanks, Skeeter!

He looked past my past and sent me on a journey that led me to where I am today. I've always been a good manager; I know now it was my healing spirit. People love working with me. Did you catch that? WITH ME, not for me. I never used the power and influence wrong; I built people up, not tear them down.

It was 2017, and I was at my wit's end; I was trying to fit in with people who didn't understand me or could relate to me and didn't like me, but I've realized it wasn't that they didn't like me. It was the light that they see in me. It is a spiritual thing. I used to think it was my size that intimidated people.

I'm 6'6" tall 250lbs and good looking lol. I've always been an overachiever. We see what we want and with God's grace I usually reach my goals.

I met a man who offered me an opportunity to switch sides and be a contractor. A remarkable woman made it a reality. 'Thank you, "Beani," Founder/Owner of Lina Bean Acadamy Tampa Florida, Lina and her team change lives for these Autistic and ADHD children. She "Walks the Talk"

Now the next two years, I learned that owning a disaster relief company was... Damn. It looked good on Facebook. I lived in Puerto Rico with a fantastic person, But I let my past and demons screw it up. Then it all came crashing down around me. I lost everything and not just my money, but a prominent man's in Wisconsin. I met Cooper on the Lake County project After Hurricane Irma came through and tore up Most of Florida. He was a self-made man. I used to wonder how a man with so much could be such a miser, but I understand now. I learned a lot from this man. It's not what you have or how much you have; It's what you do with what you have.

I've learned from the mistakes I made in Puerto Rico. My traumas and what my uncle taught me made me competitive, pride also made me careless. My actions cost me my mentor and a friend.

I went back to Jacksonville, Florida, with my tail between my legs, but it didn't last long; Hurricane Michael hit Florida's west coast, and the same man called me to come to work the storm. I was more than ready for the challenge. He started molding me into the beast I am today. I loved this family like my own. I allowed the manipulation because I was convinced, I needed him. Another symptom of abandonment issues in my life, being a people pleaser.

They treated me well, but it was toxic from that first storm; but over the years, he's gotten better, but he still hasn't realized that Karma is real.

So, he placed me on this storm, and like a whipped puppy, I kept going back, but in July 2019, I had a wake-up call.

Chapter 6
The Beginning of The End

I was helping a friend do some work on a bathroom, as we were jacking up the floor, we needed more wedges, I went out to cut a couple, and it happened so fast, the saw kicked back and snatched the wood and my hand into the blade, and my forefinger and thumb were cut off. I can still hear the pop of my fingers flapping on the saw blade.

Mark went into high gear, got me in the truck, and started to the hospital. He panicked, but he saved my life; I never knew there was a main artery in your thumb. I remember us jumping the curb near the hospital. Everything started getting bright; imagine the sun intensifying 50,000 times. I started rising out of my body; I was at peace for the first time in years.

You know that feeling when you're on a roller coaster and start going up the first climb, how slow it is, and you're anticipating the drop? It was like that, but in the blink of an eye, I woke up with the doctors around me. I asked him why it got so bright? He told me...

"You were leaving us, son." This was when the real journey started on June 29, 2019

I was released from the hospital on July 3, 2019, and I was not the same person. I started researching the reason I am alive. I was always one who stayed in my head and the past; I was my own worst enemy. I was on YouTube and found the Denzel Washington "Dream Big." I was on a mission to find the meaning of life. My dream of being a speaker started there. I've spent the last few years wondering what I would speak on, and the whole time it was me, my story. If God can use me and change me, I can give hope to who knows how many thousands of lives I can help, giving them hope.

I have found over the last few years that people are happy staying our basking in their sorrow. (Victim Mentality) and I'm not pointing any fingers as I am guilty of it too. I call it the poor, pitiful me syndrome. Not anymore.

You know we all come to earth with a gift. Once you discover your gift, you owe it to the world to give it back. We are here to learn how to love like Jesus loved while He walked on this earth.

Chapter 7
My Purpose

I have wondered for the last few years what my purpose was, then I think of all the shit I've been through, and it's an easy decision. Throughout my situation ship, I was told the stories of how their mom would make them go with these men and do sexual favors for them so she could have drugs. I mean, WHO THE FUCK DOES THAT? I know how screwed up my mind was throughout my ordeal. Can you imagine how he felt?

I mean, damn... We walk around this world and do not even realize what's happening in our neighborhoods.

So, I'm drafting this book to bring awareness to the evil and damage that is being done to our children.

With a lot of the children that have been sexually abused, me included. We confuse lust with love. I had the mindset that if someone had sex with me, I would think they loved me. I would then show what I thought was love through sex. I was confused for a long time until I got with my wife.

She would want sex 3,4 times a day. I told her I love you; I do not lust you. (It all goes back to what God revealed to me. We keep repeating the same act that traumatized us as a child.)

She did not understand, and we parted ways because I was healing; thank God she understands now. She has started the healing process.

We look at people and judge them when we know nothing about their past or the childhood traumas they have been through. We need to protect our children and if something happens and they are abused, get them help, do not brush it up under the rug because of shame and embarrassment.

Imagine what the world would be like if we healed childhood traumas. The murder rate, drug addictions, and identity crisis would be so much less. It's time for healing. I'll be damned if I want my children to go through what I've been through and watched so many others go through. It all starts with us.

Chapter 8
Suspicious Minds

How many of us daily get hurt, are taken advantage of, and abused just because we have a good heart. We want to see the best in people, and most of the time, we get hurt. I have sworn repeatedly that I'm going to be a cold-hearted bastard, and I could be for about 30 seconds; oh, it's just the heart that God gave me. I want to see the good in people. I want to believe in people, but they tend to disappoint me daily.

I spent so many years looking for love but I finally realized and listened to Spirit that I must find love in myself. Once I am happy with myself, everything else will fall into place. No one will love me as I love me, and I have to get to that point that I do love me, and you must get to the fact that you love yourself. Whether they leave or stay, it does not matter anymore because we are comfortable with ourselves and make ourselves happy. Joe Mary Todd June, they can't make you happy if you're not satisfied within yourself. Nothing or no one will ever make you happy. It is easier said than done. Let it go!

I get that message daily, but you're not seeing someone or not hearing from them. They may still have an energetic hold on you. Some people will not release, and it's like an anchor; it just weighs you down . I still tend to get suspicious, but I get suspicious whenever something true comes into my life because I have been hurt.

(We tend to allow our traumas and our thinking to self-sabotage. We create our own reality. Whatever we dwell on, is what we manifest. Negative patterns in our mindset will keep repeating. Another generational curse. Generational curses are not just physical abuse.

The mental abuse is just as traumatic. We stay in negative thinking, then our children

hear the negative talk and continue in the same pattern.)

I know you can relate. The message I got this week was, open your heart, let someone love you. I promise you I'm trying, but what is scaring me is I am getting used to being alone, and that is not good. I am not going to run after anybody anymore; there is a good mantra "I attract I don't chase, what's meant for me will simply find me." If you honestly live by this, look at yourself in the mirror every day, implement it.

It will change your life. People with good hearts there are always getting taken advantage of. We are a special breed, and even though we love a lot and share all of ourselves with someone, you can't expect them to love you as you love them. Most times it's not our heart that gets broken, it's our expectations. I speak from experience. I always expected my person to love me like I loved them. Mari broke it down to me. Some people like their sandwich made different. I like bread mayonnaise, onions then the cheese, burger mustard bread. But he liked everything on top. It's the same just put together different.

It wasn't as obvious; it did not stand out, just simple. Our traumas and just life makes us different. Just because they don't love like you expect them to. Doesn't mean they don't. My expectations fucked me up.

Chapter 9
The Awakening

July 4th, 2019, when I came home from the hospital, I had a different mindset... I had gone through Cancer Treatments with him, I'm an intuitive empath, but I did not know the difference between absorbing and acknowledging Energies. Those five weeks about killed me.

While he was going through his treatments, I absorbed his energy after he had gone through chemo, radiation, etc. So, let's recap: I've been through drug addiction, prison, heartbreak by the dozen, and near-death experience. I never say what can happen next, or things could only worsen. I don't want to think like that. So I started looking for answers. I started listening to motivational speakers; I started getting into the Tarot because it spoke to me. I hope this doesn't offend anyone, but Jesus Christ is Lord.

Often people say that people who read Tarot are of the devil; well, that's not me. I do not do anything dark. I have a spiritual gift. I'm a seer, and if I use my gift without the cards, it scares people...

My passion has been to help people and make people happy throughout my life. You know how it is. We're people, Pleasers.

If you are one of these, please stop today; people take our good hearts for granted and use them against us. I started learning about boundaries. People will only treat you how you allow them to treat you, and the ones who go throughout life helping and getting hurt and stepped on, you must learn about these things.

You must be sick and tired of being sick and tired; I started listening to the word of God a lot and different ministers and preachers and started hearing God, I started seeing Angel numbers 111 11:11 222 333, synchronicities. Sixteen signs you are having a spiritual awakening, and I'm taking this from

"Jessica Dimas' published March 29th, 2020. how to begin a spiritual awakening"

1) Acknowledge your desire

2) Recognize the nature of reality

3) Come into alignment with your desire

4) Stay in the flow.

There are so many interpretations swirling around out there about what a spiritual awakening is, and honestly, most of them don't feel so good. Spiritual Awakening, quite simply, is when you have a powerful desire and come into alignment with that desire - with your being, with the universe, with your soul.

What makes it sometimes feel like an official Spiritual Awakening is that a person will go through something painful that gives them a powerful desire for the opposite, and as they come into alignment with that desire, their perspective dramatically shifts, and they feel as if they have awoken to a new new reality.

My experience after the things that I went through. The pain and heartache the near-death. I started paying attention to the signs, numbers, and synchronicities. The funny thing about it is that it all makes sense.

We are here for a greater purpose; if humanity did what God intended us to do and that was lead with love, our world would not be the way it is today the selfishness, It's All About Me. In all reality, it is not about us. It's about loving our neighbors as we love ourselves, and this is where Karma comes in, and oh, is she sweet and sour at the same time

Chapter 10
Stuck

Have you ever been stuck?

You just have a one-track mind, and you can only think about the one thing that fucking destroyed you?

Get out of the mindset. I know it's not as easy as changing your clothes, but nothing is going to go forward until you do. If somebody wanted to talk to you.

If they wanted to text, call, reach out, come to the house, whatever... they would. So, take it for what it is; they don't give a fuck. I've been stuck for the last four years, and I say it's plum damn stupid.

I know they're thinking about me because I can feel the energy, but they enjoy that shit. So, move forward, meditate, find something else to take up your time, stay busy because you're killing yourself slowly.

I'm going to repeat myself we cannot let somebody use our love to keep us stuck and keep us in that spot, that if they decide, they'll come back, and we'll be in that same little rut. You have to love yourself enough to let go. I'm not preaching at you. I'm talking to myself too.

I came home for Thanksgiving and looked around at the same people, places, and things. They don't do it for me anymore, my family included. I'm not being cold; I'm just stating the facts.

Whenever you're in the middle of your Awakening, people also don't understand if they're not in the Awakening. You have to have faith in yourself, have faith in God / the universe puts us in situations to teach us lessons but until we learn those lessons the same thing will keep happening until you do learn your lesson. Love yourself enough to walk away, and sometimes when & if you walk away from that situation, you all could be healed.

You never know, you could get back with the same person, but you have to let go of the past hurt. Once you release the pain, you never know what the universe has planned for you. If you hold on to the hurt, pain, and what they did, you'll never heal. You must forgive them. You must forgive yourself. You must give it over to the Almighty, get out of the stuck mentality, look at yourself in the mirror every day and tell yourself. I love you. All I have focused on in the past year is finding my purpose, and I believe that telling my story here is my purpose because I know that you have been through some of the things, not all the things that I have been through. We can join together, help the universe, help the world one day at a time...

Start your day by looking in the mirror, telling yourself.

I am enough!

I am worthy!

I am love; I am lovable!

I attract, I do not chase; what is meant for me will find me.

Chapter 11
Discover your Power

Facts About Mental Health & Physical and Sexual Abuses 50% to 70% of women hospitalized for psychiatric reasons have experienced physical or sexual abuse. (Briere and Runtz, 1990) More than 1 in 4 women (27%) and 1 in 6 men (16%) experienced sexual abuse as children. (National Victim Center and the Crime Victims Research & Treatment Center, 1992).

Current estimates on the rate of child physical abuse range from 3 to 10 children per 100 children under 18. (Report of the Council on Scientific Affairs, AMA, 1993) Adult survivors of physical or sexual abuse are more likely to report depression and to have been hospitalized for depression than are other types of victims or nonvictims. A high incidence of self-destructive behavior, suicidal ideation, and deliberate self-harm (e.g., cutting, burning, or otherwise inflicting self-injury) has also been found in adult survivors of child sexual assault, distinguishing them even within clinical populations. (Council on Scientific Affairs, AMA, 1992)

Post-traumatic stress disorder is common among inpatients with a childhood sexual abuse history. (Jacobson and Herald, 1990) Physical and sexual abuse raises the risk for severe health problems. Younger girls who are physically or sexually abused often run away from home, drop out of school, engage in early sexual activity, and risk early pregnancy, HIV infection, and homelessness. (Reed, 1991)

More than 4 in every ten women reported being abused at least once before their current admission to prison. **(Bureau of Justice Statistics, 1991)**

An estimated 34% of female inmates reported being physically abused, and 34% reported being sexually abused. About 32% said abuse had occurred before they were 18 years old, and 24% said they had been abused since they were 18. (Bureau of Justice Statistics, 1991). Post-traumatic stress disorder-related flashbacks are especially prominent for sexual abuse survivors. Are post-traumatic stress disorder-related flashbacks sudden, intrusive sensory memories, often including visual, auditory, olfactory, or tactile sensations reminiscent of the sexual assault. (Briere and Runtz, 1993)

A close relative, an immediate family member, or a family friend was most often the sexual abuser for both men and women. However, men are twice as likely as women to say their abuser was a stranger. (Commonwealth Fund, 1993)

One survey showed that an overwhelming majority of women who were physically abused-92%-did not discuss these incidents with their physicians, 57% did not discuss these incidents with anyone. (Commonwealth Fund, 1993)

I have poled acquaintances in the LGBT community, and 9 of 10 were sexually abused. I have mentioned how we stay in the mindset of repeating what traumatized us.

I was made to do oral on my rapist. So, I always thought if I did that, then that showed love, and if I did it good then they would love me. I had an encounter with a man, he did not want that. I found myself not interested in the act of homosexuality. God has shown me that I am not a homosexual. My trauma says that I am. The attraction to men that I have had all these years comes directly from my trauma. On dating LGBT dating apps, if a man hits me up, one of the first questions is. How big is it? I have been in situations where my partner was Anally raped, and the only thing that satisfied them was to be penetrated by size that physically hurt them. If we are honest with ourselves. The only satisfying part of a homosexual relationship is reliving the trauma.

The subconscious mind is destroying us. Healing is what we need. When I mention this. People want me silenced. I have tried to help the one who raped me. He just stays drunk, and his family enables him to stay in his drunken Stuper. They hate me, with my spiritual gift I read energy, I am a human lie detector. I am a alchemist **(Alchemy is defined as a "divine secret" that is** inherited from our father Adam, who passed it on to his sons the wizards and the philosophers of Islam, through honorable awliya' (saints) and the great prophets" The work goes on to Divide alchemy into two sciences: The elixir, which deals with them "fixing of the corrupted,")

The best way I know how to describe it is when I walk into a negative situation and transmute the energy, dissolve the negative and turn it into positive.

Like walking into the fighting ring and instead of blows to the head, you give hugs from the heart. If you don't feed the negative and nurture the positive, the negative will die and the good will grow. We come to earth to learn how to manipulate energy, and love like Jesus loved.

On the cross, what did He pray?

"Father, forgive them. For they know not what they do." He prayed for the men who were murdering him.

Love is the answer to all things.

Chapter 12
Self-Love What It Means

Before a person can practice it, we need to understand what it means. Self-love is a state of appreciation for oneself that grows from actions that support our physical, psychological, and spiritual growth. Self-love means having a high regard for your well-being and happiness.

Self-love means taking care of your own needs and not sacrificing your well-being to please others. Finally, self-love means not settling for less than you deserve.

Self-love can mean something different for each person because we all have many ways to take care of ourselves. Therefore, figuring out what self-love looks like for you as an individual is an essential part of your mental health. Put the phone down, connect to yourself or others, or do something creative. Eating healthily, but sometimes indulging in your favorite foods.

Self-love means accepting yourself as you are in this moment for everything you are. It means accepting your emotions for what they are and putting your physical, emotional, and mental well-being first.

So now we know that self-love motivates you to make healthy choices in life. When you hold yourself in high esteem, you're more likely to choose things that nurture your well-being and serve you well. These things may be in the form of eating healthy, exercising, or having healthy relationships. Becoming mindful. People who have more self-love tend to know what they think, feel, and want.

Taking actions based on need rather than want. By staying focused on what you need, you turn away from automatic behavior patterns that get you into trouble, keep you stuck in the past, lessen self-love, and practice good self-care. You will love yourself more when you take better care of your basic needs.

People high in self-love nourish themselves daily through healthy activities, like sound nutrition, exercise, proper sleep, intimacy, and healthy social interactions.

Making room for healthy habits. Start truly caring for yourself by mirroring that in what you eat, how you exercise, and what you spend time doing. Do stuff, not to "get it done" or because you "have to," but because you care about you.

Finally, to practice self-love, start by being kind, patient, gentle and compassionate to yourself, the way you would with someone else that you care about.

Chapter 13
The Eye of The Storm

It was September, and Hurricane Laura hit Lake Charles Louisiana, my Call to Duty. I've been doing disaster relief since Hurricane Matthew in 2016. My friend, my family, Johnny Diamond "this guy is the storm God" I met during Hurricane Irma. He gave me advice, told me what to do, and a dear friend Lina who believed in me provided my bucket truck.

I went to work as planned, and on paper, it looks good but making it happen…Now that's another story.

I struggled. I'm glad my uncle made me the man I am because I'm of the mind that you can't beat me, and I refuse to let anything beat me. So, it all started there, and three storms later found me in Lake Charles Louisiana.

It wasn't like other storms. It was the worst I have seen. I honestly had never seen a storm like this. We were riding one day, and Johnny showed me what needed to be done; he said to put together some teams and Get'er done. This is yours...

I don't think he realized at the time what was going to happen on this job. Out of nowhere, it got stupid overnight. We started a little cliché, but it took us by storm. I have never had, nor did I ever dream that the money running through my business was real. When I tell you it was life-changing, it was life-changing. If you want to call it an overnight success, wow, but enough about that, money makes people change.

It taught me a valuable lesson. Money does not buy happiness. It brings greed, and hatefulness; don't forget the haters.

People don't want to see you do good. They would rather you stay the loser or somebody they can talk about.

I love to see people succeed, but I guess it's because of my heart. But it taught me more than one lesson you can be foolish with it, and I lost a chunk. Even though I made a lot, I lost a piece from being careless, not paying attention, and not being prepared.

One thing that didn't change was my love for Mari. So around January 2021, I invited him to come to Lake Charles, and I thought we had a breakthrough; never go against your gut.

The day I pulled up, he had his suitcases and the dog. I love that dog. Caramel, a Red Nose Pit, and Chihuahua mixed. She was so precious, and she loved her master no matter what. It was the happiest day of my life.

I was finally going to get them away from all this toxicity in Jacksonville, Florida, and we would start a new life; that is what was running through my head. We were going across this long ass bridge going into Louisiana it's like six miles. He looked at me and tears were running down my face. I had never been so happy in all my life. He got my mind right lol. He never has been with the emotional thing.

He grabbed my hand and held it for a while which shocked me, but I just cherished the moment. In Jacksonville I was never able to really see the real Mari unless we went to our duck off spot in Ponte Vedra. He was so amazing.

It didn't take long for the craziness to start.

They never video chatted with me for five years, but there was one guy; they video chatted. Oh, we are just going to play games together, yeah, I know it. But the icing on the *cake* was whenever they said that their uncle had died and I wasn't going to take him back,

but then I said, you know what? I'm not a selfish bastard, and we planned, and on the way back, he was drinking.

Finally, he got a phone call and three words that I had only heard twice in a couple of years; he said it to him he said I love you too.

My heart was destroyed; I knew that I had been played once again. People use your love to kill you. Facts are facts; he was there to teach me a lesson, and I have never loved anything in life more than him. We were two damaged people, And I chose to heal, and he did not. I went from Victim mode to survivor. It all goes back to childhood traumas.

You can look at it from two angles Because empaths draw narcissists to them - the wounded stay in abusive relationships. Well, I decided to choose myself and stop the madness. I learned my lesson. It felt like my heart was being ripped out of my chest, but had I not walked away, the universe would have kept giving me the same situation until I finally learned my lesson.

Chapter 14
His Will

"I want you to understand in this age and era, where our comfort has become so important, that there are times in life that God doesn't care that you are not comfortable. He cares about His purpose for your life, He cares about His will, He cares about our destiny, but God doesn't always care about your comfort. Being in the will of God will make you uncomfortable.

If you don't believe it, ask Jesus about the cross. (TD Jakes)" those bumps in the roads were there for a reason.

Paul told the men on the boat, whenever they were panicking, that an angel had come to him and said he had to stand trial in Rome; they asked what that meant, Paul? He declared, "you won't die because I'm on the boat" (Acts 27: 24-26). A lot of you all won't catch this, but your family, your friends, and people in your surroundings would treat you better if they only understood that the favor of God on your life is the reason they are blessed. If you're wondering why you always come out of situations unscathed, it's because God's favor is on your life.

He'll direct our path in uncomfortable ways when we get off course.

We all come to earth with a gift; once we find out what that gift is, we owe it to the world to give it back.

"God doesn't make mistakes, and if He called you into that position no matter how overwhelming the position is, it's because he believes that you are the woman or the man for the job, and so our task then becomes to ask God what is it that You know about me that would have you place me in this position because if you place me in this position then you know something about me that I don't know yet and sometimes our greatest prayer should be God would you open up my eyes so that

I can see whom I am supposed to be in your kingdom that I would not compare myself to everything that came before me or the things that are coming up behind me but that I would trust that you placed me in this position because no one else can do it like me" { Sarah Jakes Robert's) God didn't bring you this far to leave you. God is able, God is good, God is great, God is merciful, God is forgiving, God is powerful, God is everything, say amen if you believe.

Chapter 15
A New Beginning

Today I chose myself! Many people say that they choose themselves, but how true is it?

We say it, but we still allow people to drain our energy and steal our power. So, you must learn what "boundaries " really mean.

(Personal boundaries are the physical, emotional, and mental limits we establish to protect ourselves from being manipulated, used, or violated by others.

They allow us to separate who we are and what we think and feel from the thoughts and feelings of others.)

I found that when I started setting boundaries, two things happened.

1. People started falling away and leaving my life.

2. I became the crazy one. Everyone swore that I had lost my mind and was crazy and then proceeded to leave my life.

I have had to walk away from the love of my life; at one time in my life, I would have rather died than let them go, but I had to choose me because loving them was killing me. My own family was just as toxic. You'll learn that the people closest to you don't want to see you better yourself. It's the cold hard truth that you must be ready to accept if it happens. When you're elevating, not everyone can go with you. It's hard to walk away from people, places, and things, but it's necessary.

Chapter 16
Obedience

I got a message tonight. God said to write down everything that was stolen from me, including my crown.

1. My childhood: my innocence.

2. My self-esteem

3. My dignity

4. My peace

5. Self-worth

6. by singing career.

7. My children

8. My respect

9. Love

10. Trust

11. My Crown

"Lord, I trust you, and today I'm picking up my cross and following You." I've fought for the last four years to get my life together. Next chapter, it'll become clear. It wasn't for nothing; my experiences—and—pain-will help many, and I'm grateful that He's made it clear that He knew I was strong enough to carry the load.

Take a minute to write down what you have lost. Or what the enemy has taken from you.

God will give you back tenfold.

What the enemy has stolen from you. It's healing time. It's time to take our power back. We must let go of the pain.

Let go of the past, move forward, and make sure that our children do not *go* through the hell we went through.

It all starts with us breaking generational curses and exposing family secrets.

Chapter 17
Family Secrets

Every family has its secrets. Maybe the child, as in my case, was raised by an aunt & uncle or grandparent, and the reason was never discussed. Others could be sexual abuse that got swept up under the rug, physical abuse they swept up under the rug, or like in most cases, just emotional abuse the trauma that carries over into our teenage years, most of the time, we stay in abusive relationships and then pass it on to the next generation. It's time we take a stand.

Chapter 18
Decide

I have a question for everyone, yes you. When will you decide to protect your peace and your child's peace, don't be ignorant of the world around you or stay ignorant to the life of hiding Our family secrets and curses?

This is my pledge to expose all violations in my family and yours. I refuse to stand by and watch another generation of trauma and abuse go unnoticed.

For hundreds of years, mental and physical abuse has been Brushed up under the rug like it never happened. Instead, we take the pain and anguish into our future and mask it or drown out the sound with alcohol, drugs or stay in the energy of abusive relationships and continue the cycle of abuse onto' our next generation.

2022 we will bring worldwide attention to the skeletons in your closet and mine. Imagine the world healing and preventing all or most childhood trauma in the world... Can you imagine the energy or frequency of the earth?

Just think of the happiness you see in your child's eyes... Can you see it? Now do your duty! Protect it ' It starts with the person in the mirror.

Let's take a stand and end the generational curses that have haunted our families for generations. It's healing time!

Chapter 19
Final Thoughts

I sit here thinking that there is so much more to say about life's path. But you know when a toddler starts walking, they take baby steps...One step at a time. Healing is a process that's not going to happen overnight. I will make a worksheet titled 100—Shadow-Work—Prompts.

It is not for the week at heart. But it is challenging Because it calls you to face your demons and childhood traumas to help heal the inner child.

At the end of it all, you will become a better, complete human being. This is meant to be life changing.

I am grateful to all that take the time to read my story, and I pray that it helps you on your journey. The next time Someone asks how you are doing? You let them know   "I am moving forward."

My heart will never be the same

In January 2022, I came home from Atlanta. I had left Louisianna and had my sons in Atlanta for a little while. We had our Christmas early and I took them back on December 23, 2021. I drove back to Atlanta with a heavy heart. I slept all day Christmas. I was forced to close my business because I was losing my eye site. I have Macular degeneration, I am fifteen years too young to have it but life is life. I came home I got us a house. We stayed in the In Town Suites for a couple of weeks while I was having some remodeling finished. Mari came and helped me organize my office and cooked dinner; He was exhausted.

It had been five months since I had seen him. After I brought him back February of 2021, his health went down. I got word he was in the hospital, so I flew home and went to see him. He screamed at me, and I went to leave but he asked me to stay. He had lost 40lbs.

He asked me? "Why are you staring at me?" I said, "because you're so beautiful." He just shook his head. I have never seen anyone as beautiful as him. I see the real him, beyond the physical. We talked for a while, and I left and cried on the way back to the airport.

Whie he was organizing my office I told him I was going to get his mom a house. He said, "No the fuck you're not either!"

I explained he could move in at our house, so I could take care of him. He said, "I can't leave Zye," his little brother. His phone had been ringing for a couple of hours, he ignored it. His mom called my phone eventually and I took him home. He would come and help me clean over the next couple of months.

He called me one afternoon and we went to mom's and seen her. We went back to the house, and he cooked us dinner and once again I took him home.

I continued in my everyday routine of staying to myself and finishing this book. I have been used and had my love used against me for so long. God had separated me and had been revealing who the people

in my life truly were. It was heart breaking. At the end of May Mari had called and asked if I wanted to chill. He came to the house. It was different, it's like he had transformed. He was affectionate, he lay on my chest facing me and was making plans for us to be together.

He kissed me more times in 10 minutes than he had in 5 years, which threw up red flags. He told me "You are going to be number one!" I was angry and I replied, "bitch I'm going to be the only one or nothing at all!"

I had never talked to him like that. This is the person I would have died for. Then his phone rang, and the man on the other end asked.

"Where the fuck you at?" I guess he didn't realize I could hear the conversation. I stood up and told him to get his shit, let's go. He looked at me with alarm on his face. I had never stood up to him before, I had always accepted the manipulation, but I was done, he cried all the way back to his mom's.

He apologized for all the times he had hurt me. I had made my decision. I refuse to let my love destroy me anymore. I was relieved but my love was still strong for him, but my boundaries were set.

July 14, 2022, I was sitting at my desk. I mentioned earlier in the book of our telepathic connection, and something told me to call the hospital. I did and he was there. I went straight to room 710. I walked in and it was dark. I went to turn the light on and he said no, he had a migraine. So, I asked him what was wrong, he said "cancer" He was fine when he was at the house.

We talked for a second and I started towards the bed, and he stopped me, He had his little attitude and he said, "will you leave? I asked. "Will you call me when you get home?" and he said "yes" I told him" "I love you" and I left. It was normal for him to run himself down and he would be in the hospital for a few days and then go home.

The following Friday at 7:32 am my phone rang, and it was his friend Ja'Quaid and he said Mari's mom just called him and told him about Mari. I asked, "What about him?" My brain knew what it was, but my heart wasn't accepting. He said Mari had passed away at 7:10am. I couldn't breathe. It was like someone punched me in the stomach.

This could not be happening. I have never felt such pain in my life. I cried every day for 5 months; my family has never seen me like this. As I am writing now tears are flowing down my face. I never got to say goodbye. He died alone; his own family didn't care enough to be there. I would have been there.

A few months after it was revealed to me.

When God wants to bless you, what does He do?

He sends people into your life.

When Satan wants to distract or destroy you. What does he do?

He sends people into your life.

I had a picture blown up and I made a frame to take to the funeral home because I did not expect his mom to have an open casket. On my way to the funeral home, I heard God's voice say, "I'm going to show you what he was on the inside!"

I walked into the funeral home to take the picture in, and I had a white rose. I was told how he had transformed within minutes of his death. He was so beautiful, but what was in that casket looked like a dried-up demon, I was already crying but I almost collapsed. I placed the rose on his chest. It fell to his side, and I cringed because I did not want to touch that thing in the casket.

When God tells you to let go of the past. I beg you do not test Him; I have seen His wrath. I had never feared God until then.

We all have a calling. To fulfill God's purpose in our life. Sometimes He must crush us, to turn our pain into power and push us into our purpose.

I really hope my story will help you seek God and seek healing, as I would never wish this pain on anyone. I will continue to seek justice for Mari and all children of sexual abuse. He did not deserve the pain and anguish he went through. If I can save one child from this, I have accomplished something, but if we join, we can save thousands.

Do not ignore the abuse that happens every day in our community.

I'll always Love You

D'Marius "Mari" Carter

Chapter 20
100 Shadow Work Prompt

Psychoanalyst Carl Jung popularized the idea of the shadow self, and according to neuroscientist Tara Swart, Ph.D., it's composed of the parts of yourself that you reject. The term 'shadow' is used to describe personality aspects that we have repressed in our lives, mostly in childhood. For example, as a child, you may have been scolded for being too outspoken, so there's a chance that you won't feel safe speaking your mind from that point on.

Shadow work means bringing the repressed personality parts back into consciousness, learning to accept and love them. Uncovering, welcoming, and integrating shadows lead to emotional balance and inner freedom. Combining our shades teaches us to love ourselves unconditionally with all our supposed flaws and weaknesses.

"Until you make the unconscious conscious, it will

direct your life, and you will call it fate." -Carl Jung.

Pay attention to your triggers: Carl Jung said, " Everything that irritates us about others can lead us to understand ourselves." What bothers you about others is usually a quality you suppress within you.

Reward yourself: Shadow work is not easy and offering compassion to those parts of ourselves that we have hidden away for so long is essential. It is okay to take a break occasionally, if we can bounce back.

Seek professional help if needed: If confronting the shadow sides of yourself brings about pain, suffering, or fear that you feel ill-equipped to handle, I would advise you to seek the help of a licensed professional.

100 shadow work Prompts

What is the Shadow?

The idea of the shadow self was popularized by psychoanalyst Carl Jung and according to neuroscientist Tara Swart, PhD, it's composed of the parts of yourself that you reject. The term 'shadow' is used to describe personality aspects that we have repressed in the course of our lives, mostly in childhood. For example, as a child, you may have been scolded for being too outspoken so there's a chance that you won't feel safe speaking your mind from that point on.

What is Shadow Work?

Shadow work means bringing the repressed personality parts back into consciousness, learning to accept and love them. Uncovering, accepting and integrating shadows leads to emotional balance and inner freedom. By integrating our shadows, we learn to love ourselves unconditionally with all our supposed flaws and weaknesses.

"Until you make the unconscious conscious, it will direct your life and you will call it fate." **-Carl Jung**

When doing Shadow Work:

-Pay attention to your triggers: Carl Jung said " Everything that

irritates us about others can lead us to an understanding of ourselves."

What bothers you about others is usually a quality within you that you surpress.

-Reward yourself: Shadow work is not easy and offering compassion to those parts of ourselves that we have hidden away for so long is important. It is okay to take a break every once in a while, if we can bounce back.

-Seek professional help if needed: If confronting the shadow sides of yourself brings about pain, suffering or fear that you feel ill-equipped to handle then I would advise you to seek the help of a licensed professional.

1. IF YOU COULD SAY ONE THING TO THE PERSON WHO HAS HURT YOU
2. THE MOST... WHAT WOULD YOU SAY & WHY?
3. WHAT IS YOUR BIGGEST FEAR? WHY?
4. WHERE IN YOUR LIFE ARE YOU CURRENTLY FEELING THE MOST
5. ISOLATED & HOW ARE YOU DEALING WITH THAT?
6. WHAT EMOTION DO YOU DEAL WITH IN A SELF-DESTRUCTIVE WAY?
7. HOW DO YOU USUALLY DEAL WITH THIS EMOTION?
8. WHAT DO YOU HATE ABOUT YOURSELF? WHY & WHO TAUGHT YOU TO HATE IT?

9. ONE THING YOU GENUINELY LOVE DOING? WHY DO YOU LOVE DOING IT? WHY DON'T YOU DO IT MORE?

10. ONE THING SOMEONE TOLD YOU THAT COMPLETELY DISCOURAGED

11. YOU? WHY DID IT DISCOURAGE YOU?

12. LIST 20 THINGS YOU LOVE ABOUT YOURSELF. WRITE AN APOLOGY LETTER TO YOURSELF FOR FORGETTING THESE THINGS.

13. WHAT IS SOMETHING YOU CURRENTLY ENVY IN SOMEONE ELSE'S LIFE & WHY? WHY DO YOU WANT THIS THING SO BADLY? WHY DOES IT MAKE YOU JEALOUS OF THIS PERSON?

14. NAME THE LAST CRUEL THING YOU SAID TO SOMEONE FOR THE PURE

PURPOSE OF MAKING THEM FEEL BAD
ABOUT THEMSELVES.

15. EXPLORE THE FEELINGS BEHIND
WHAT YOU SAID.

16. WRITE OUT THE WORDS YOU NEED TO
HEAR TODAY.

17. WRITE ABOUT SOMETHING YOU HATE
ABOUT YOUR PAST. HOW HAS IT HELD
YOU BACK IN LIFE? WHERE HAS IT
HELD YOU BACK?

18. WHAT EMOTION ARE YOU MOST
AFRAID OF FEELING & WHY?

19. WHAT IS THE GREATEST HEARTBREAK
YOU'VE SUFFERED & IN WHAT WAYS
WERE YOU RESPONSIBLE?

20. LIST 1 THING YOU HATE ABOUT
YOURSELF. HOW DOES THIS HATRED
NEGATIVELY IMPACT YOUR LIFE?

21. WHAT FRIENDSHIP/RELATIONSHIP DO YOU HOLD ONTO THAT IS UNHEALTHY FOR YOU? HOW WOULD RELEASING THEM BENEFIT YOU?

22. LIST THE WAYS YOU ARE PRIVILEGED. WHAT DO YOU TAKE FOR GRANTED?

23. WHAT WAYS DO YOU SHOW UP FOR OTHERS BUT FALL SHORT FOR YOURSELF?

24. WRITE A LETTER TO YOUR MOTHER YOU WISH SHE COULD

25. HAVE READ BEFORE VOU WERE BORN.

26. WRITE A LETTER TO YOUR DAD YOU WISH HE COULD HAVE READ

27. BEFORE YOU WERE BORN.

28. IN WHAT WAYS DO YOU REGULARLY DISAPPOINT YOURSELF? WHY

29. ARE YOU DISAPPOINTED?

30. IF YOU COULD DELETE ONE MEMORY, WHAT WOULD IT BE & HOW

31. WOULD YOU NO LONGER BE AFFECTED?

32. WHAT IS ONE THING YOU COULD DO IN YOUR DAILY LIFE TO HEAL YOUR INNER CHILD?

33. WHAT BRINGS YOU PEACE? WHY DOES IT BRING YOU PEACE?

34. HOW DO YOU FEEL WHEN SOMETHING DOESN'T TURN OUT THE WAY YOU WANT?

35. HOW LONG DOES IT TAKE FOR YOU TO GET OVER YOUR MISTAKES? WHY DOES IT TAKE THAT LONG?

36. ARE YOU HONEST WITH YOURSELF ABOUT YOUR FEELINGS?

37. DO YOU FORGIVE EASILY?

38. HOW DOES IT FEEL TO HAVE YOUR EMOTIONS BELITTLED OR DOWNPLAYED?

39. WHAT ARE YOU HOLDING ONTO? WHY ARE YOU HOLDING ONTO IT? HOW ARE YOU HOLDING ONTO IT?

40. WHAT ASPECTS OF YOUR LIFE NEED TRANSFORMING?

41. WHAT'S THE BIGGEST LIE YOU'VE EVER TOLD TO YOURSELF AND SOMEONE ELSE?

42. WHAT ARE YOU MOST AFRAID OF FINDING OUT ABOUT YOURSELF?

43. WHAT ARE YOU MOST AFRAID THAT SOMEONE WILL FIND OUT?

44. WHAT MAKES YOU THE HAPPIEST?

45. HOW JUDGED DO YOU TEND TO FEEL ON A DAILY BASIS? EXPLORE HOW MUCH OF THAT PERCEIVED

JUDGEMENT IS REAL AND HOW MUCH IS IMAGINED

46. YOUR ABSOLUTE DREAM LIFE: HOW DOES YOUR PERFECT DAY BEGIN?

47. DO YOU PROJECT CERTAIN ASPECTS OF YOURSELF ONTO OTHERS?

48. DID YOUR PARENTS PROVIDE YOU WITH ALL YOU NEEDED?

49. WRITE ABOUT THE LAST TIME YOU RAN AWAY FROM YOUR RESPONSIBILITIES. CONSIDER WHY YOU DID THAT AND WHAT THE RESULTS WERE.

50. WHAT DO YOU THINK ARE THE WORST CHARACTER TRAITS A PERSON CAN HAVE? WHEN IS A TIME YOU HAVE DEMONSTRATED THESE TRAITS)

51. WHO HAS THE MOST INFLUENCE OVER YOU? IS IT HEALTHY?

52. HAVE YOU FORGIVEN ALL THE PEOPLE WHO HAVE HURT YOU?

53. WHAT THINGS ARE TRIGGERS FOR YOU? CONSIDER WHERE THOSE IRRATIONAL FEELINGS STEM FROM.

54. DO YOU REWARD YOURSELF WHEN YOU ACCOMPLISH SOMETHING POSITIVE?

55. WHEREABOUTS DO YOU TEND TO EXPECT OTHER PEOPLE TO CONFORM TO YOUR BELIEFS? WHAT SCARES YOU THE MOST ABOUT ALLOWING PEOPLE TO HAVE THEIR OWN BELIEFS IN THAT AREA?

56. WHEN YOU THINK ABOUT YOUR FUTURE, WHAT ARE YOU MOST AFRAID OF?

57. WHAT IS IT YOU WOULD LIKE TO HEAL FROM?

58. WHAT DO YOU STRUGGLE THE MOST WITH & HOW CAN YOU FIX THIS?

59. WHO ARE YOU? WHO DO YOU WANT TO BECOME?

60. WHAT IS LOVE IN YOUR OWN DEFINITION?

61. WHAT MISCONCEPTION DO PEOPLE HAVE ABOUT YOU? HOW DOES THAT MAKE YOU FEEL?

62. HOW IMPORTANT ARE YOU TO YOURSELF? HOW HIGH DO YOU PRIORITIZE YOURSELF? HOW DO YOU RATE IMPORTANCE?

63. HOW DO YOU THINK PEOPLE SEE YOU? HOW WOULD THEY DESCRIBE YOU HOW DO YOU FEEL ABOUT THAT?

64. THINK OF A RELATIONSHIP YOU'VE WALKED AWAY FROM. WRITE (DOWN

THE REASONS IT'S BEEN A POSITIVE LIFE CHOICE.

65. WHAT DRAINS YOUR ENERGY?

66. WHAT MEMORIES BRING YOU SHAME? THINK ABOUT WHO YOU

67. WERE THEN, WHAT LED TO YOUR BEHAVIOUR, AND HOW YOU'VE CHANGED SINCE.

68. WHAT ARE YOUR PARENTS' BEST/WORST ATTRIBUTES? HOW ARE YOU ALIKE/UNLIKE THEM?

69. WHAT EMOTIONS TEND TO BRING OUT THE WORST OF YOU? WHY DO THINK THAT IS?

70. WHO HAS LET YOU DOWN THE MOST IN YOUR LIFE? ARE THEY STILL AROUND? HOW DO YOU FEEL ABOUT THAT?

71. WHAT IS THE WORST EMOTION SOMEBODY COULD PROVOKE IN YOU?

72. WHY DO YOU FEEL SO STRONGLY ABOUT THIS? DOES YOUR ANSWER DIFFER ACCORDING TO THE PERSON IN THE QUESTION?

73. HOW DOES DRAMA MAKE YOU FEEL? ARE YOU DRAMATIC YOURSELF? DO PEOPLE CALL YOU DRAMATIC? HOW DO YOU FEEL ABOUT THIS?

74. HOW DO YOU VIEW ASKING FOR HELP? IS IT A SIGN OF STRENGTH OR WEAKNESS? WHY IS THIS?

75. WHAT MAKES YOU SELF-CONSCIOUS AROUND OTHERS?

76. WHAT DOES FREEDOM MEAN TO YOU?

77. WHAT IS YOUR BIGGEST STRUGGLE IN LOVING YOURSELF? HOW COULD YOU WORK WITH IT MORE?

78. WHAT SONG DO YOU HAVE AN EMOTIONAL CONNECTION TO? WHAT EMOTIONS COME TO YOU WHEN YOU PLAY IT?

79. WHAT NEGATIVE EMOTIONS ARE YOU MOST COMFORTABLE FEELING? HOW OFTEN & WHY DO THESE EMOTIONS SHOW UP DAILY?

80. WHAT ARE YOU THANKFUL FOR?

81. WHAT ARE YOUR THREE BIGGEST GOALS?

82. WHAT IS SOMETHING YOU'LL NEVER FORGET?

83. WHAT IS THE BIGGEST PROMISE YOU MADE TO YOURSELF THAT YOU'VE BROKEN?

84. HOW DO YOU LIE TO YOURSELF IN DAILY LIFE? WHAT ARE YOU TRYING TO AVOID?

85. WHICH OF MY WEAKNESSES COULD ACTUALLY HAVE POTENTIAL?

86. HOW WOULD YOU DESCRIBE YOURSELF TO A STRANGER?

87. WHAT DO YOU NEED TO STOP RUNNING AWAY FROM?

88. WHY ARE YOU NOT LIVING TO YOUR HIGHEST POTENTIAL? WHAT IS HOLDING YOU BACK?

89. WHAT CAN'T YOU ACCEPT ABOUT YOURSELF? WHY CAN'T YOU ACCEPT IT?

90. WHAT ARE YOU IN CONTROL OF AT THIS MOMENT? WHAT DO YOU WANT TO BE IN CONTROL OF? WHY?

91. DO YOU FEEL SAFE IN THIS WORLD? DO YOU FEEL SAFE IN YOUR BODY? WHY/WHY NOT?

92. HOW MUCH DO YOU JUDGE OTHERS ON A DAILY BASIS? WHAT DO YOU JUDGE THEM FOR?

93. WHAT IS SOMETHING YOU WOULD NEVER TELL ANYONE ELSE?

94. WHO HAVE YOU BEEN PRETENDING TO BE?

95. WHAT IS YOUR DEFINITION OF SUCCESS?

96. WHAT ARE YOUR GREATEST GIFTS/TALENTS? HOW ARE YOU CULTIVATING THEM IN YOUR LIFE AND IN THE LIVES OF OTHERS?

97. WHAT CAN YOU DO DAILY TO BECOME YOUR HIGHEST SELF?

98. WHAT FICTIONAL VILLAIN/ANTI-HERO DO YOU MOST RELATE TO?

99. WHAT ASPECTS OF YOUR PERSONALITY IS THE CHOICE BASED ON?

100. WRITE ABOUT A TIME YOU CHOSE NOT TO FORGIVE SOMEONE. WHY DID YOU NOT FORGIVE THEM?

101. WRITE A LETTER TO YOURSELF (OLDER/YOUNGER/CURRENT-YOU DECIDE)

102. WHAT ARE YOU MOST PROUD OF YOURSELF? AND OTHERS?

103. WHAT QUALITIES DO YOU ADMIRE IN OTHERS?

104. ARE YOU OPEN TO OTHERS ABOUT YOUR EMOTIONS AND FEELINGS?

105. WHY/WHY NOT?

106. WHO DO YOU IDOLISE AND PLACE ON A PEDESTAL?

107. WHAT EXPERIENCES LEAD TO DDISSOCIATING& ESCAPE FROM REALITY?

108. HOW CAN YOU ADD MORE POSITIVITY TO YOUR LIFE?

109. WHAT DO YOU MISS ABOUT CHILDHOOD?

110. IN WHAT AREAS OF YOUR LIFE ARE YOU HOLDING BACK AND PLAYING SMALL? WHEN DO YOU FEEL SMALL AND WEAK?

111. IF THE DARKER PARTS OF YOU WERE TO SPEAK THEIR TRUTH RIGHT NOW, WHAT WOULD IT SAY?

WRITE A LETTER TO THE UNIVERSE LETTING GO OF ANY FEELINGS AND MEMORIES THAT ARE HIDDEN. LET GO OF ANYTHING THAT IS NO LONGER OF ANY USE TO YOU. BURN IT, THROW IT AWAY OR KEEP IT

Since I released this book, a lot has changed. This is an insert from my blog on my website iammovingforward.net

Am I the only one who feels this way?

I have cried so hard the last 3 weeks, it's insane.

Can you imagine being on a rollercoaster ride for 5 years? That is what my life has been, straight, confusing insanity that was out of control. Hello everyone, I'm JJ. Welcome to I Am Moving Forward. Healing is an ongoing process. Self-love is a daily practice. I was in a situation ship, for the last 5 years. "The Biggest Lesson of My Life".

I have a question for you.

When God wants to bless you. *What does He do?* (He sends people into your life)

When Satan wants to distract you. *What does he do?* (He sends people into your life)

101

Shadow work saved my life. Had I not been in the latter prompts of shadow work, I might have entertained the thought of eating a bullet.

The person I fell so deeply in love with. The one I would have died for. He passed away a month ago. It hit me harder than i could have ever imagined...

I had learned boundaries, and had broken it off, i severed the energetic cord that bound us. I took my power back 5 weeks before his death.

It was the hardest pill that I had ever swallowed when it was revealed to me that he was my distraction. When God has a purpose for your life, and you get the message... Let go of the past!!!

Please heed the warning.

Then the one thing that loved me more than life. My Chihuahua. Bryan who I called "Bubbas" He died 3 days ago. I can't even explain or describe the pain that was chewing up my soul. My thoughts are. God has a purpose. better said "I'll find purpose in the pain"

I said all of that to tell you this. Everything happens for a reason, and God or Satan put's people in your life for a reason if only for a season. I've learned my lesson.

Life comes in cycles, either you learn, or you keep repeating the cycle until you do. I hope this reaches who it is supposed to reach. It's Healing Time.

No one wants to admit the pain or confusing thoughts that run around in our minds daily. It happens to all of us. Childhood Traumas are real. I started I Am Moving Forward, to be that listening ear, that shoulder and the guide that can quiet the thoughts, and self-sabotaging self-talk that is hindering us from moving forward and living our best life. I love you and the Lord loves you. May you be blessed and hope to hear from you soon.

Since July I have been searching for answers and I have tested the waters, even on myself.

I met someone and spent some time with them, to get my mind off grief.

As a child I was molested and was made to do oral on my offender. Throughout my life that is the only thing I focused on as I confused lust with love, and I was convinced if I did that on my mate, that was showing love.

On the LGBT dating apps, I have found that one of the first questions I get or others also. How big is your private part? If the person was anally raped as a child.

The only thing that satisfies them is physical pain when they are penetrated. It all comes down to feeding our traumas. The subconscious mind is winning. There is no happiness in a homosexual lifestyle. In my experience, it's only been drama, fighting and infidelity. Sex is the only thing that is important.

No one wants intimacy, as most homosexuals that I've dealt with are emotionless. No love and after they climax, they don't want to be touched. They want to get high, have sex and move on to the next person. I know I'll get a lot of dissension from this but if they are honest with themselves.

They know I am right "It's Healing Time!!"

JJ Snipes

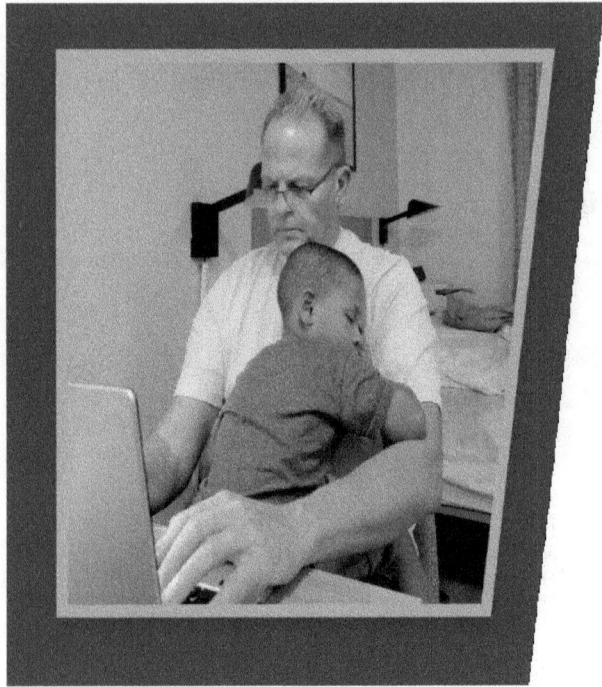

One night while drafting this book, my son woke and crawled in my lap and fell back asleep. My nephew took the picture.

About the Author

JJ was born in the wee hours of the morning May 24th, 1971, in Jacksonville Fla. He was raised by his Aunt Sissy& Uncle Lefty. Throughout his life singing and music was an outlet that helped him through the tough times. His passion was always helping people and making them laugh. He decided to tell his story after a near death experience in 2019. In hopes that his story can help others start the healing process from childhood traumas.

www.ingramcontent.com/pod-product-compliance
Lightning Source LLC
Chambersburg PA
CBHW061753020426
42331CB00006B/1456